ENGLISH PUNCTUATION

Robyn Gee and Carol Watson

Designed and illustrated by
Kim Blundell

Contents

With thanks to Diccon Swan  Centre, University of Reading.

What is punctuation?

Punctuation is a collection of marks and signs which break words up into groups and give other helpful clues and information about their meaning. The purpose of punctuation marks is to make it easier for people to understand the exact meaning of written words.

This book explains the different uses of each punctuation mark and gives lots of tips and hints on how and where to use them. Here, you can see the complete range of punctuation marks to choose from.

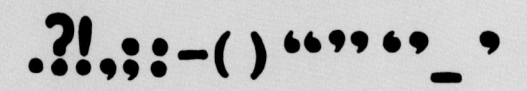

It might help you to understand exactly what punctuation marks do if you think about the difference between spoken words and written words.

When someone speaks they can do all sorts of things to help make the meaning of their words clearer to the person or people listening to them. They can vary their voice by making it higher or lower, or louder or softer; they can change the tone (or quality) of their voice and the speed at which they speak; and they can put in pauses of various different lengths. If the person listening can see, as well as hear, the person speaking, the expression on the speaker's face and the gestures they use, it can also help to communicate the exact meaning of their words.

Most people, without even thinking about it, use all these techniques to help them express the meaning of their words. In other words, these things act as "voice punctuation". When people don't use voice punctuation they are boring to listen to and difficult to understand. When children first learn to read aloud they usually ignore voice punctuation and this makes it hard to follow the meaning of the words they are reading.

Written punctuation cannot convey as much as voice punctuation, but it is still very important. It tells you how to turn the words into the right voice patterns to help you understand them. Today, once people have learnt to read, they usually do this inside their heads, but back in the Middle Ages anyone who could read and understand something without reading it aloud, or at least mouthing it, was considered very rare and talented.

Helping you read

One important thing that punctuation tells you is when and how long to pause when you are reading. The number and length of the pauses can make a great difference to the meaning of the words. You can see this by comparing the meaning of the two sentences below.

> **Charles I walked and talked half an hour after his head was cut off.**

> **Charles I walked and talked. Half an hour after, his head was cut off.**

At one time people used to write without putting any gaps between words. They then began to realize how helpful it would be to separate groups of letters into words, so that they could be converted back into speech more easily. The next step after separating the words was to put in punctuation marks for the pauses.

> **Atonetimepeoplewrotewithout puttinganygapsbetweenwords**

If you listen to people talking you will probably notice that their voices rise at the end of a question, but fall at the end of most other sentences. You can test this by getting someone to read the sentences below.

> **This is the best you can do.**

> **This is the best you can do!**

> **This is the best you can do?**

The rise and fall of a voice is called its intonation pattern and is often an important part of the meaning of spoken words. (In some languages, such as Chinese, the same word said with different intonations can mean totally different things.) Punctuation marks, especially question and exclamation marks, indicate what intonation you should use.

Are there any rules?

There are very few unbreakable rules of punctuation. Once you have learnt the basic uses of each mark, the way you punctuate can often be a matter of what you happen to prefer. Remember that there is often more than one perfectly correct way of punctuating a sentence. Concentrate on the clearest, simplest way of expressing something. The main thing to remember is

Is it useful?

that each mark should be useful. If a punctuation mark is not doing anything useful, leave it out.

When you are having difficulty trying to decide which punctuation marks to use in something you have written, it can be very helpful to say the words aloud and think about the pauses you use when you say them. A tape recorder can be even more helpful. It is very good practice to record yourself, or someone else, describing a scene or incident. Then play back the

recording, writing out your own words and putting in punctuation wherever you paused. Play back the recording again and check your written version against it.

In this book the main guidelines on how to use punctuation are given in the text. Examples which help to illustrate these guidelines are surrounded by blue borders.

> **She had a blue- eyed, big-eared, bird-brained boyfriend.**

Remember the capital letters

A team of little punctuation experts make comments and suggestions to help pick out particular points. The English used in books, newspapers and magazines sometimes follows slightly different rules and conventions from those described in this book, so don't worry if you see things in print which you would express differently in writing.

Test yourself

There are short tests on each section. These appear in yellow boxes so that you can spot them easily. There are also two pages of tests and quizzes on pages 26 and 27. The answers to all the tests are on pages 28 to 31. Always do the tests on a separate piece of paper.

In some sections you will find "Do" and "Don't" boxes. The "Don't" boxes warn of common mistakes and pitfalls to avoid. The "Do" boxes summarize the main points to remember about the more complicated punctuation marks.

Punctuation is very closely linked to grammar (the rules about the way words are used in a language), so you may come across the occasional grammatical term (e.g. "noun", "clause"). If you do not understand any of these terms or feel a bit hazy about the meaning, turn to the glossary on page 32 to check the exact meaning.

Full stops

Full stops (also called full points) do several jobs. They are the strongest punctuation mark, making the most definite pause.

1

They are used at the end of all sentences which are not questions or exclamations. (A sentence is a word, or group of words, which makes complete sense on its own.)

2

The witch stirred the cauldron.

This is a sentence

Stop.

Hello.

These are one word sentences.

Sentences usually have a noun and a verb, but they can, sometimes, consist of only one word.

3

Who are you?

Help!

A sentence can also be ended by a question mark, ? (see page 6) or an exclamation mark, ! (see page 7). In these cases you don't need a full stop.

4

The boy sat up. He got out of bed.

Don't forget the capital letter.

When you have used a full stop to end a sentence, remember to start the next sentence with a capital letter.

Stop the everlasting sentence

Remember the capital letters.

This is a very long sentence which does not make any sense. Can you put it right? There should be five full stops.

He trudged wearily along the dusty road his feet hurt and his head throbbed there was not a soul in sight for miles and he wondered what to do next then he saw someone waving at him at the top of the hill it was a tall man in a large hat

Three full stops in a row

You can use three full stops where part of a quotation or text is left out.

"Jack and Jill went up the hill . . . and Jill came tumbling after."

You can also use three full stops to show where a sentence is unfinished.

"He hid behind the gravestone and . . ."

I wonder what happened?

Notices, lists and labels

You don't use full stops in these.

No full stops here.

NO ENTRY

EXIT

PEKING
PARIS
ATHENS
TOKYO
ROME
MOSCOW

MINT

TOFFEE

Shortening words by using full stops

Instead of writing some words in full you can cut them short, or "abbreviate" them, by just writing some of the letters, or just the first (initial) letters.

A full stop is used to show where letters have been left out, words shortened, or after initials.

Feb. 14th
Sun. 30th

Prof. (Professor)
Rev. (Reverend)

You can use a full stop to shorten the names of the days of the week and the months of the year. It is also used to shorten titles.

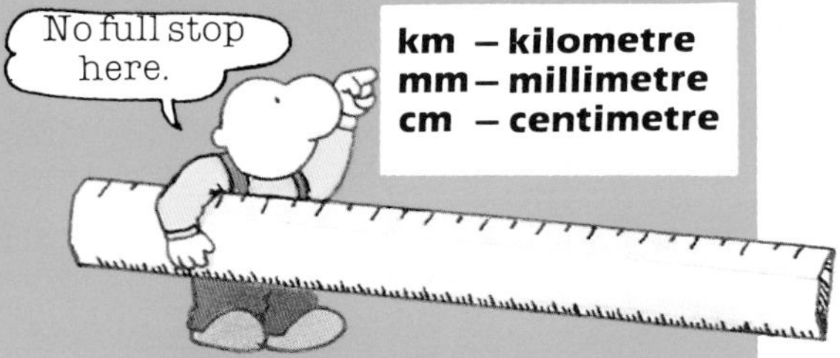

Dr – Doctor
Mr – Mister

Where the first and last letters in the shortened form are the same as in the full word, you can leave off the full stops if you want to.

No full stop here.

km – kilometre
mm – millimetre
cm – centimetre

Don't use full stops with abbreviations of metric measurements.

Joanna Jane Johnson
J. J. Johnson

Sometimes the first (initial) letter of a word is used to stand for the whole word. People's first names are often written as initials.

If an abbreviation comes at the end of a sentence, you don't need to use two full stops.

UN   **(United Nations)**
NATO **(North Atlantic Treaty Organization)**
BBC   **(British Broadcasting Corporation)**
USA   **(United States of America)**

No full stop here.

You can leave out the full stops after initial letters of well-known organizations and place names.

► **They took the dog to the R.S.P.C.A.**

Short or long?

These words can be written in a much shorter way. How can you abbreviate them?

Victoria Cross
et cetera
Reverend John Williams
Professor Alexander
Johnson
Saint Augustine
centimetre

Do you know what these abbreviations stand for?

| A.A. | R.A.C. | Y.W.C.A. | R.S.P.C.A. |

| W.R.V.S. | St. John Ch. 4 v. 3 | B.Sc. |

You may need a dictionary.

5

Question marks

A question mark is used at the end of a sentence which asks a question. It is used instead of a full stop so the next word begins with a capital letter.

When the word or words in the sentence actually form a question it is called a *direct question*. This kind of sentence expects an answer.

> **Which is the best route to London?**

An *indirect question* is a sentence which does not ask a question but tells you what question was asked. It does not have a question mark.

No question mark here.

> **He asked which was the best route to London.**

A question can be just one word.

These are questions

Why? **Who?** **How?**

When? **What?**

Take care! If a sentence begins with one of these words it does not necessarily mean it is a question.

but this isn't.

> **When it is cold I wear my hat.**

Uncertainty

Sometimes a question mark is used to show doubt about something like a date of birth. These should not be used in normal writing.

Question tags

A question can be tagged on to the end of a sentence.

> **It's not far, is it? I can get there tonight, can't I?**

Question quiz

Which of these sentences do you think are questions?

1. Where is the hotel
2. He asked how much it would cost
3. Is it expensive
4. Will I like the food
5. What an awful room
6. It's a large room, isn't it
7. How long shall I stay

Exclamation marks

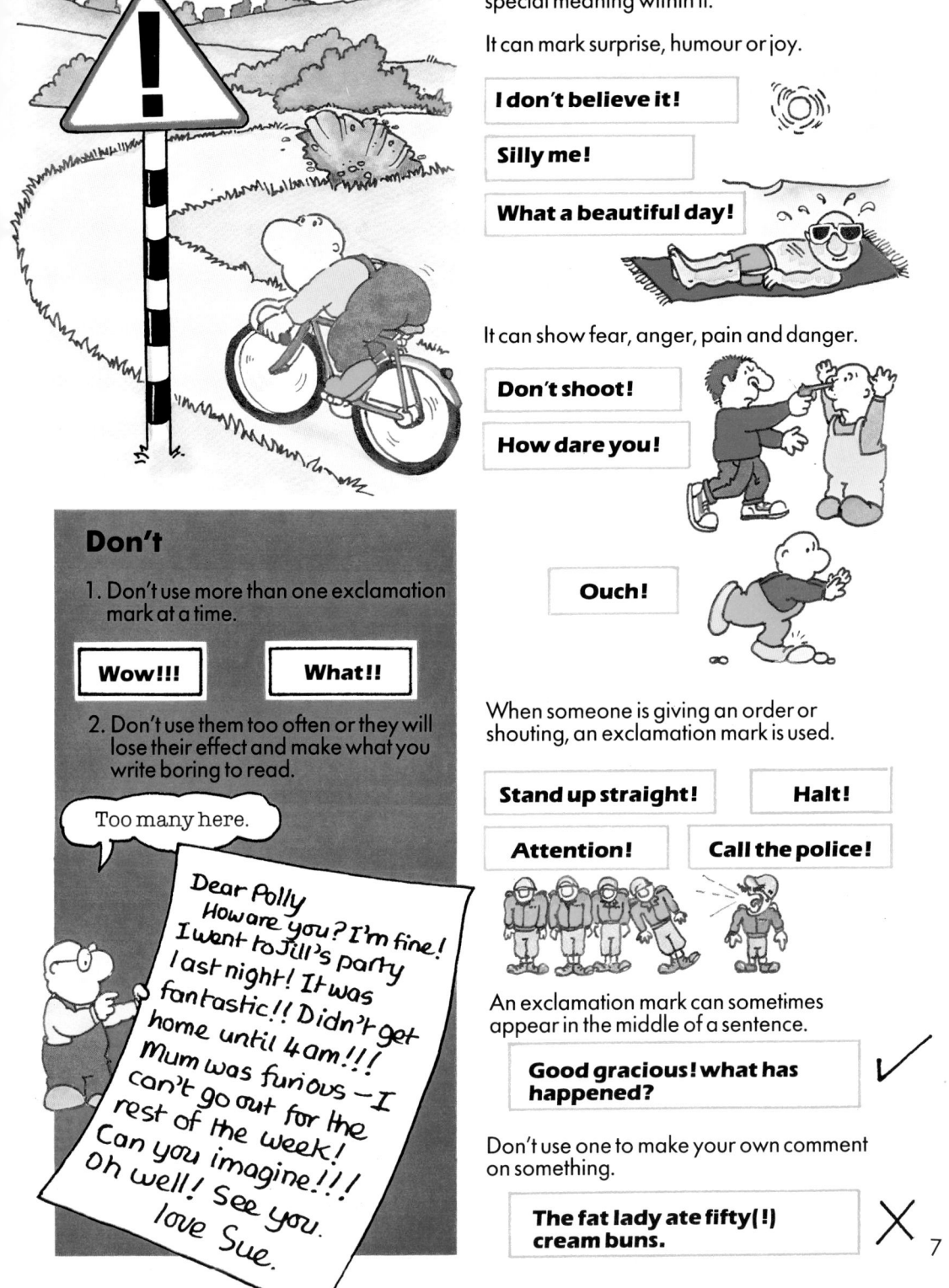

An exclamation mark is used at the end of a sentence or phrase to emphasize some special meaning within it.

It can mark surprise, humour or joy.

> **I don't believe it!**

> **Silly me!**

> **What a beautiful day!**

It can show fear, anger, pain and danger.

> **Don't shoot!**

> **How dare you!**

> **Ouch!**

Don't

1. Don't use more than one exclamation mark at a time.

> **Wow!!!**   **What!!**

2. Don't use them too often or they will lose their effect and make what you write boring to read.

Too many here.

Dear Polly
How are you? I'm fine!
I went to Jill's party
last night! It was
fantastic!! Didn't get
home until 4 am!!! —
Mum was furious — I
can't go out for the
rest of the week!
Can you imagine!!!
Oh well! See you.
love Sue.

When someone is giving an order or shouting, an exclamation mark is used.

> **Stand up straight!**   **Halt!**

> **Attention!**   **Call the police!**

An exclamation mark can sometimes appear in the middle of a sentence.

> **Good gracious! what has happened?** ✓

Don't use one to make your own comment on something.

> **The fat lady ate fifty(!) cream buns.** ✗

7

Commas

We ate chocolate, jelly and cake.

This makes it sound as though the jelly was made of chocolate.

We ate chocolate jelly and cake.

A comma is used to mark a brief pause, much shorter than a pause made by a full stop. It can be used to separate two words, or groups of words, in a sentence, in order to make the meaning clear.

Commas are the most common punctuation mark, but you have to be careful how you use them. You can easily change the meaning of a sentence by moving a comma to a different place or taking it away altogether.

Lists

When there is a list of words in a sentence, each word in the list is separated from the next by a comma.

They may be nouns,

We will need hammers, nails and a saw.

The last word in the list is usually joined to the the list by "and", instead of a comma.

or adjectives,

Mr Cherry was a warm, hospitable man.

or verbs.

She stopped, stared and ran.

The list may consist of groups of words divided by commas, instead of single words.

Sam frightens the cat, teases the dog, bullies his brother and annoys the neighbours.

There is no comma before the first word in the list, or after the last.

Try these

Can you see where the commas should be?

All these sentences need commas to help clarify their meaning. Can you see where they should be?

1. The monster was huge fat and spiky.
2. Everyone threw spears stones swords and boiling oil at the creature.
3. It roared growled spat and groaned but still it did not die.
4. A knight appeared wearing bright shining armour and pierced the beast with his special magic sword.
5. The huge beast screamed fell to the ground rolled over and died.
6. The king rewarded the knight with gold silver diamonds rubies and other precious things.

Long sentences

1

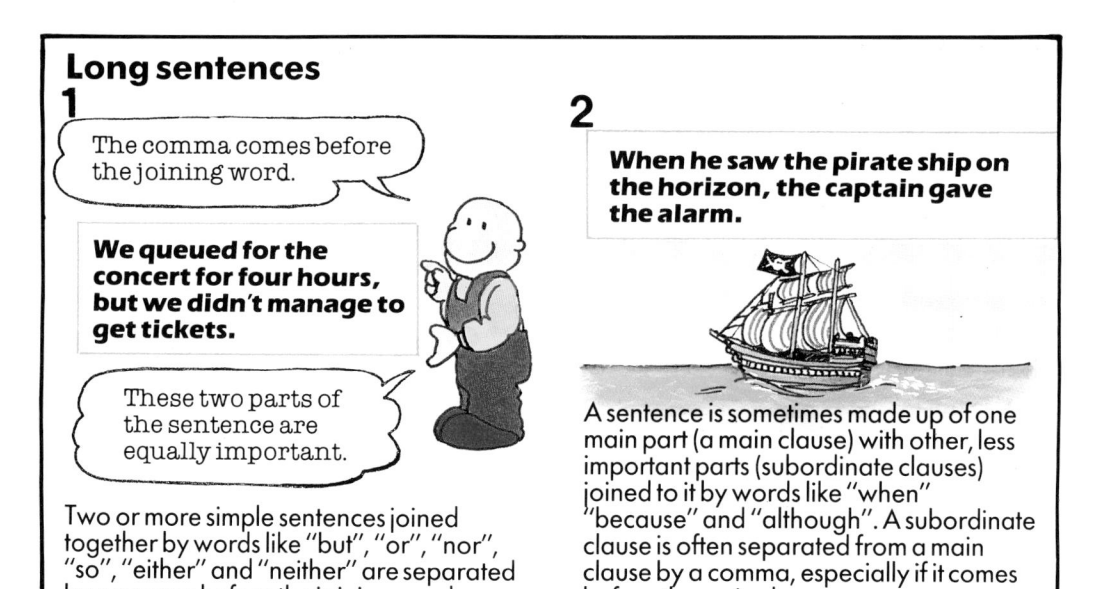

The comma comes before the joining word.

We queued for the concert for four hours, but we didn't manage to get tickets.

These two parts of the sentence are equally important.

Two or more simple sentences joined together by words like "but", "or", "nor", "so", "either" and "neither" are separated by a comma before the joining word.

2

When he saw the pirate ship on the horizon, the captain gave the alarm.

A sentence is sometimes made up of one main part (a main clause) with other, less important parts (subordinate clauses) joined to it by words like "when" "because" and "although". A subordinate clause is often separated from a main clause by a comma, especially if it comes before the main clause.

Sentence linking words

The joining words in long sentences are called conjunctions. Here are some more common conjunctions:

Beware! Some of these words are not always conjunctions.

after	if
before	unless
until	though
while	as
since	for

When you see any of these words think about using commas to separate the group of words they introduce from the rest of the sentence.

Commas with "and"

Commas are not generally used with "and". In a list "and" tends to replace the comma, but sometimes you need to use a comma before "and" to make the meaning absolutely clear.

The best horses in the race were Pacemaker, Starlight, Mr Speedy, Windstorm, and Thunder and Lightning.

Without this comma you might think there were four horses, or that the fourth horse was called Windstorm and Thunder.

Test yourself

Use the information above to help you.

Can you improve these sentences by adding commas?

1. The robber climbed through the window crept up the stairs and peered into the bedroom.
2. She called as loudly as she could but no-one could hear her.
3. The telephone was not far away yet there was little she could do to reach it.
4. She switched on all the lights so the man ran away in a panic.
5. The policeman who arrived later told her to put a lock on her window.

Inessential words and phrases

Commas are used to separate words or phrases in a sentence. The words enclosed by the commas could be left out without changing the general sense of a sentence.

Try reading these sentences through, then read them again, leaving out the words surrounded by commas.

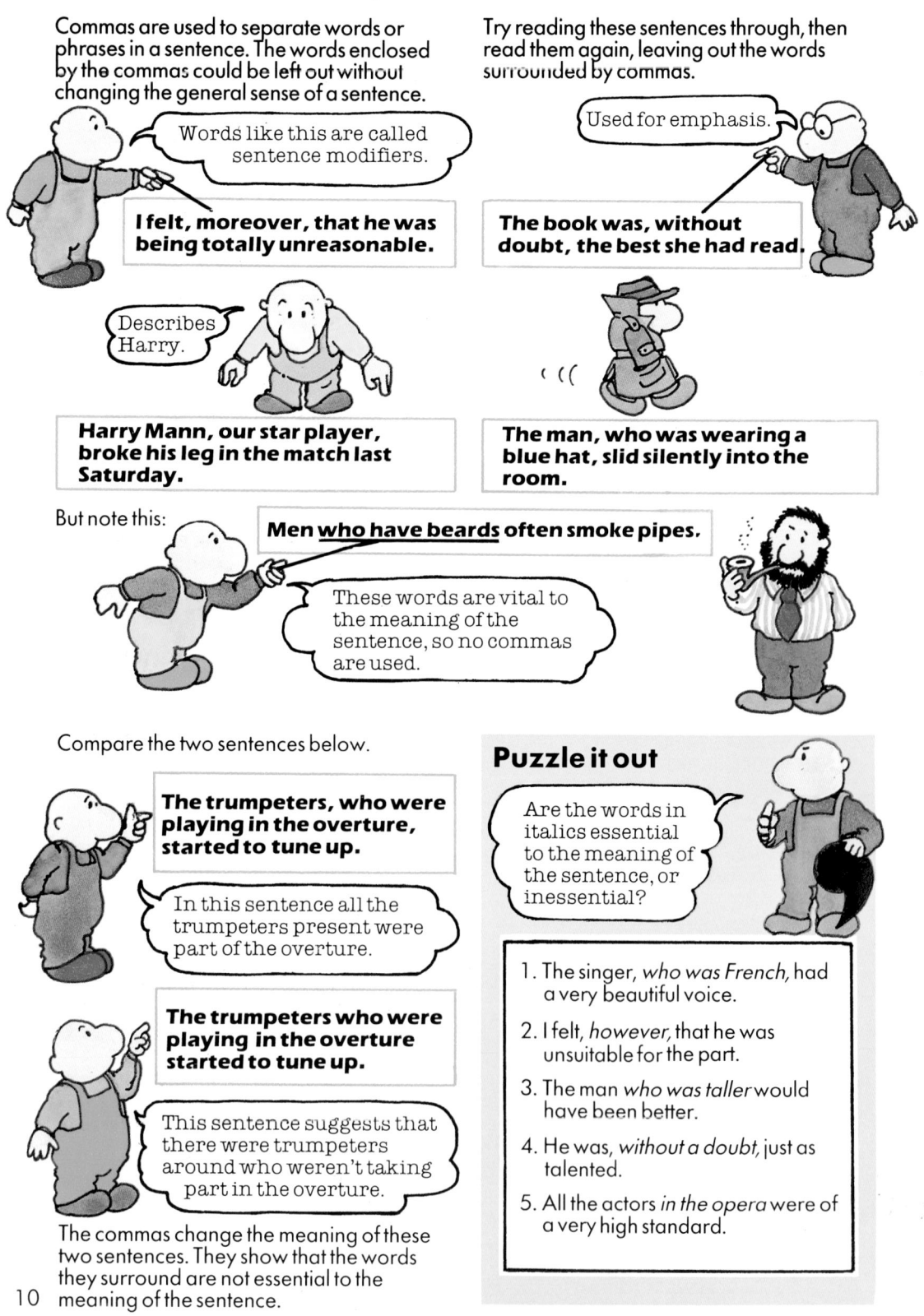

Words like this are called sentence modifiers.

I felt, moreover, that he was being totally unreasonable.

Used for emphasis.

The book was, without doubt, the best she had read.

Describes Harry.

Harry Mann, our star player, broke his leg in the match last Saturday.

The man, who was wearing a blue hat, slid silently into the room.

But note this:

Men <u>who have beards</u> often smoke pipes.

These words are vital to the meaning of the sentence, so no commas are used.

Compare the two sentences below.

The trumpeters, who were playing in the overture, started to tune up.

In this sentence all the trumpeters present were part of the overture.

The trumpeters who were playing in the overture started to tune up.

This sentence suggests that there were trumpeters around who weren't taking part in the overture.

The commas change the meaning of these two sentences. They show that the words they surround are not essential to the meaning of the sentence.

Puzzle it out

Are the words in italics essential to the meaning of the sentence, or inessential?

1. The singer, *who was French,* had a very beautiful voice.

2. I felt, *however,* that he was unsuitable for the part.

3. The man *who was taller* would have been better.

4. He was, *without a doubt,* just as talented.

5. All the actors *in the opera* were of a very high standard.

Addresses and letters

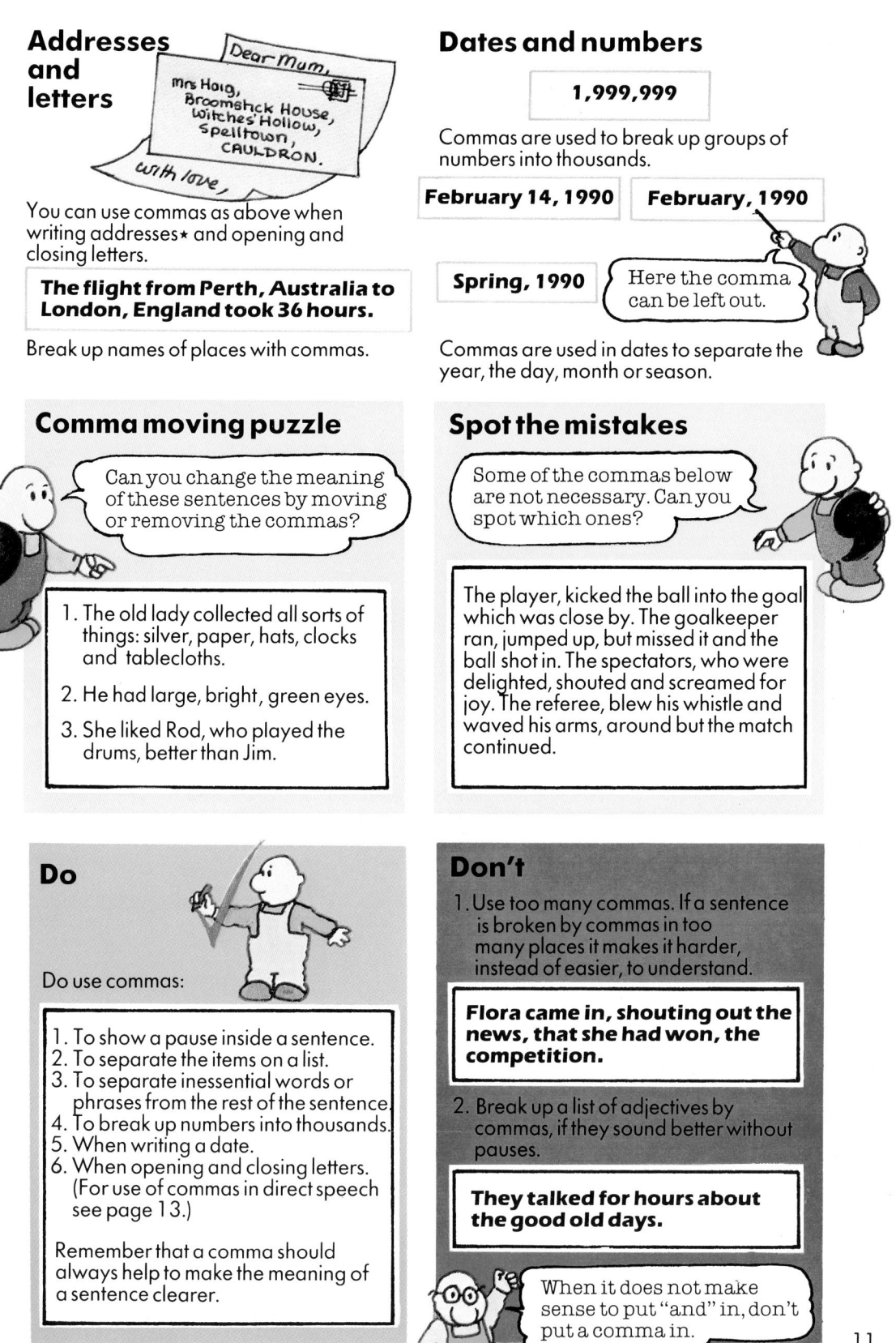

Dear Mum,

Mrs Haig,
Broomstick House,
Witches' Hollow,
Spelltown,
CAULDRON.

with love,

You can use commas as above when writing addresses★ and opening and closing letters.

The flight from Perth, Australia to London, England took 36 hours.

Break up names of places with commas.

Dates and numbers

1,999,999

Commas are used to break up groups of numbers into thousands.

February 14, 1990   **February, 1990**

Spring, 1990   Here the comma can be left out.

Commas are used in dates to separate the year, the day, month or season.

Comma moving puzzle

Can you change the meaning of these sentences by moving or removing the commas?

1. The old lady collected all sorts of things: silver, paper, hats, clocks and tablecloths.

2. He had large, bright, green eyes.

3. She liked Rod, who played the drums, better than Jim.

Spot the mistakes

Some of the commas below are not necessary. Can you spot which ones?

The player, kicked the ball into the goal which was close by. The goalkeeper ran, jumped up, but missed it and the ball shot in. The spectators, who were delighted, shouted and screamed for joy. The referee, blew his whistle and waved his arms, around but the match continued.

Do

Do use commas:

1. To show a pause inside a sentence.
2. To separate the items on a list.
3. To separate inessential words or phrases from the rest of the sentence.
4. To break up numbers into thousands.
5. When writing a date.
6. When opening and closing letters. (For use of commas in direct speech see page 13.)

Remember that a comma should always help to make the meaning of a sentence clearer.

Don't

1. Use too many commas. If a sentence is broken by commas in too many places it makes it harder, instead of easier, to understand.

Flora came in, shouting out the news, that she had won, the competition.

2. Break up a list of adjectives by commas, if they sound better without pauses.

They talked for hours about the good old days.

When it does not make sense to put "and" in, don't put a comma in.

★See page 25.

Inverted commas

Inverted commas are also called quotation marks, quotes or speech marks. They are used in writing to show the exact words that someone has spoken. This is called direct speech.

Spoken words.

Inverted commas always appear in pairs.

Spoken words can be set out in three basic ways:

they can come at the beginning of a sentence,

"I have won a holiday for two in France," said Fred.

they can come at the end of a sentence,

Fred said, "I have won a holiday for two in France."

Use inverted commas only around the words actually spoken.

or they can come at the beginning and end of a sentence with an interruption in the middle.

"I have won," said Fred, "a holiday for two in France."

Make the inverted commas curved and facing inwards.

Capital letters

A capital letter must be used whenever someone starts to speak,

Capital letter.

Alice asked, "How did you manage to win a holiday?"

but do not use a capital letter unless it either starts someone's spoken words or starts a sentence.

No capital letter.

"How," asked Alice, "did you manage to win a holiday?"

Reported speech

There are two ways of writing down what someone says. You can write down the person's exact words (direct speech) and put them in inverted commas, or you can report what they said in your own words. The second way is called reported or indirect speech. With reported speech you do not use inverted commas.

"I have always wanted to go to France," said Alice.

Alice said that she had always wanted to go to France.

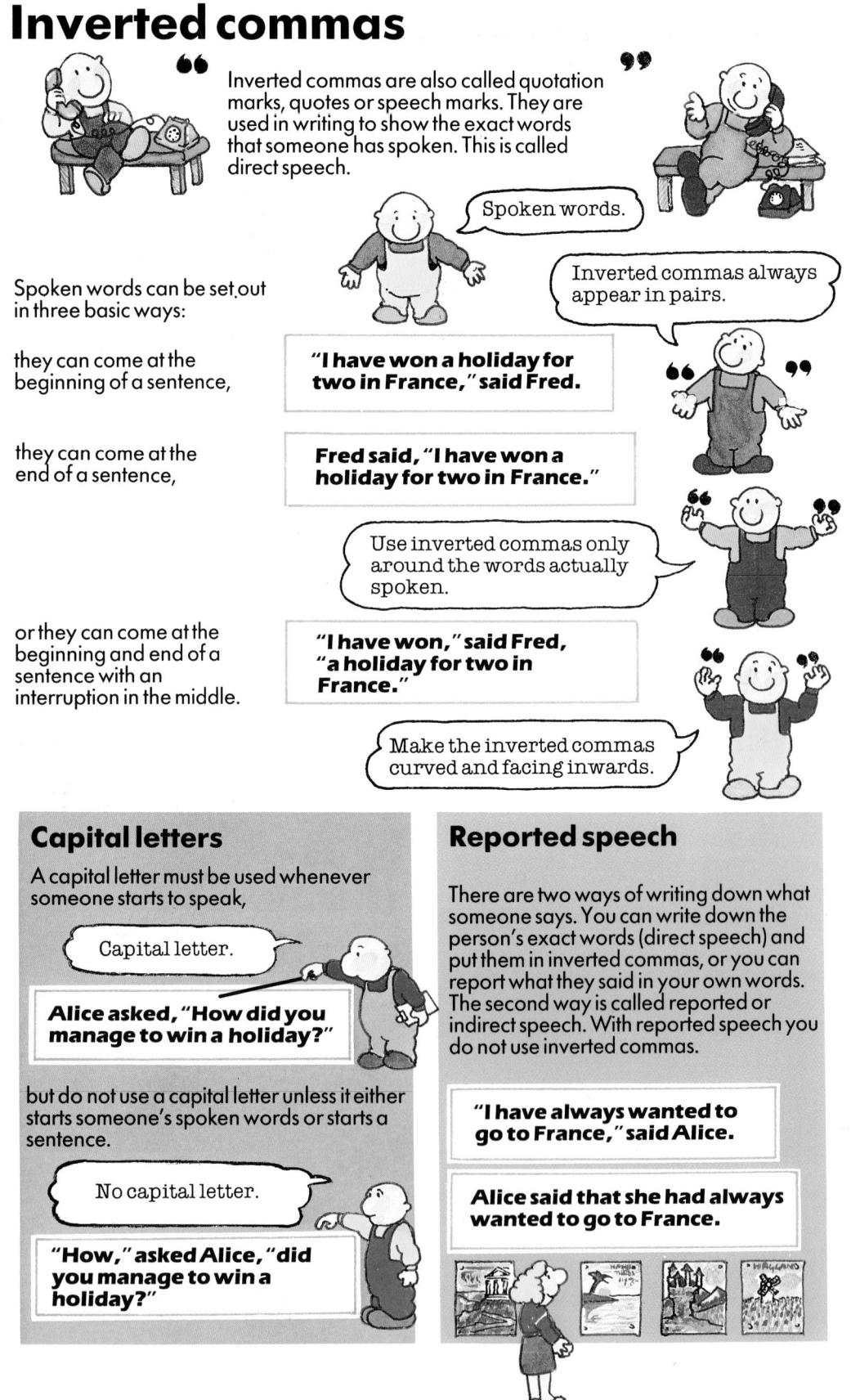

Commas with inverted commas

In direct speech there must always be a comma between the introduction to speech (subject and "verb of saying") and the speech itself.

The verb of saying is often "says" or "said", but all these can be verbs of saying:

mutter	ask	declare
whisper	reply	comment
cry	exclaim	observe
shout	repeat	command

When the words spoken come before the verb of saying, they are followed by a comma,

"I am very excited about going abroad," said Fred.

The comma goes inside the inverted commas.

but if the words spoken are a question or exclamation, use a question mark or an exclamation mark, not a comma.

"When are you going?" asked Alice.

"You lucky thing!" she said.

When the verb of saying and its subject start the sentence, they are followed by a comma.

Fred replied, "We are leaving tomorrow morning."

The comma goes before the inverted commas.

The first word spoken has a capital letter.

When the spoken sentence is interrupted to insert a verb of saying and its subject, one comma is needed before breaking off the spoken words and another before continuing.

This comma goes inside the inverted commas.

This comma goes in front of the second pair of inverted commas.

"I do hope," said Alice politely, **"that you and your friend have a wonderful time."**

This word is continuing the spoken sentence so it starts with a small letter.

Remember, also, to use commas:

round people's names, when they are spoken to by name,

► **"I was wondering, Alice, if you would like to come with me,"** said Fred.

round words like "yes", "no", "please" and "thank you",

► **"Yes, of course I would."**

before question tags.

► **"But I can't be ready to leave tomorrow morning, can I?"**

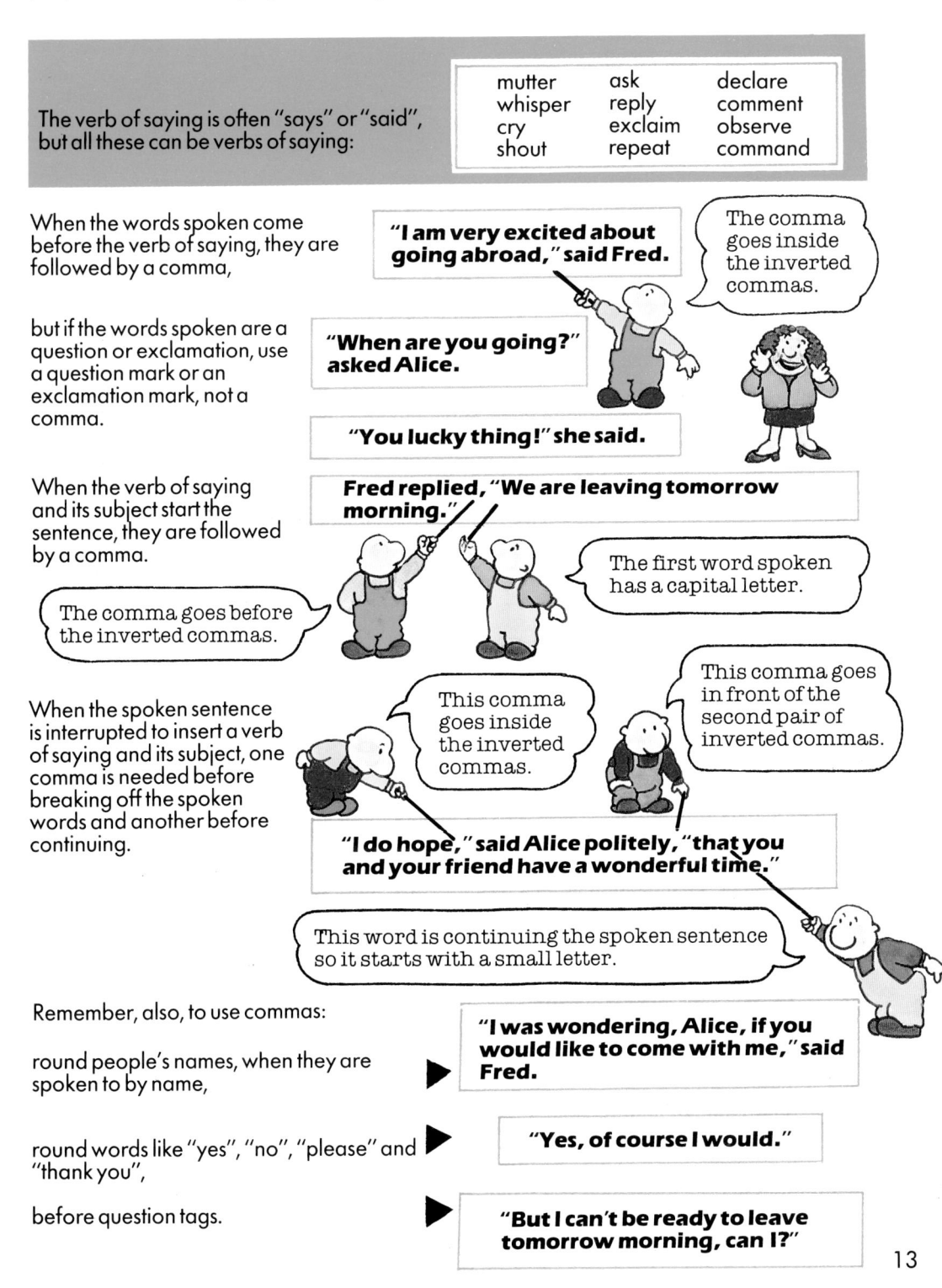

Punctuation patterns to remember

If you find it difficult to decide what punctuation marks to use with inverted commas and what order to put them in, the punctuation patterns below may help you. Look at all the different patterns and decide which one best suits the sentence you want to write. The red block represents the spoken words; the blue block represents the verbs of saying.

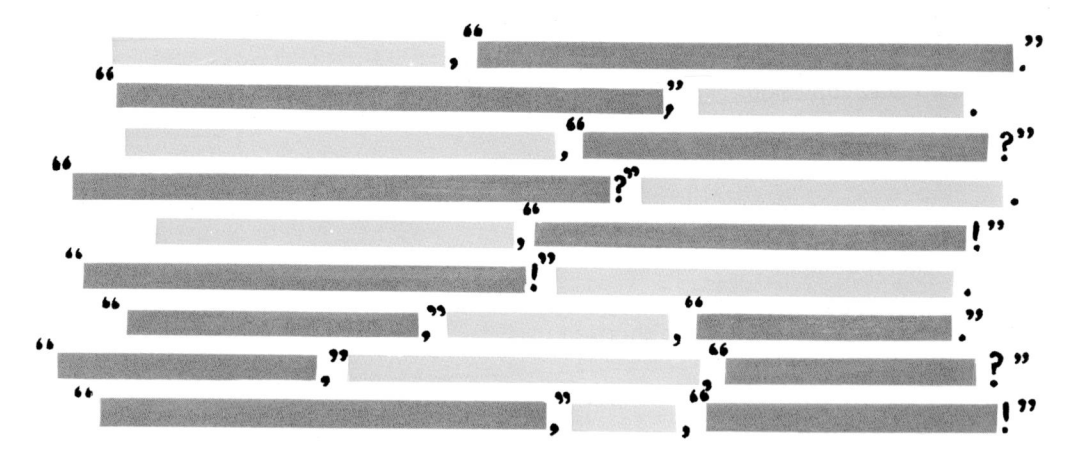

Commas, full stops, question marks and exclamation marks after spoken words usually come inside the closing inverted commas.

Turn nonsense into a conversation

(When you use inverted commas for a conversation always start a new paragraph when one person stops speaking and another starts.*)

Good morning, how are you today? the doctor asked. I feel dreadful, he replied gruffly. You should try to get up and walk about, she suggested. Then you might feel better. You must be joking! he exclaimed. Do you want a patient or a corpse?

Quotations

Pages 12 and 13 explain how inverted commas are used when you are quoting (repeating the exact words) that someone has said. They are also used when you quote the exact words from a book, newspaper or magazine.

Use full stops to show where you have left out some of the original words.

"One day. . . I was exceedingly surprised with the print of a man's naked foot on the shore, which was very plain to be seen in the sand." This was when Robinson Crusoe first realized there was another human on his island.

You must also use inverted commas when you quote a proverb or traditional saying.

Some people feel that "many hands make light work", but in my experience "too many cooks spoil the broth".

14

*See page 24.

Single inverted commas

> 'I have nothing to declare except my genius,' he said.

You can use single inverted commas instead of double ones, but single ones look rather like apostrophes,* which can cause confusion.

> "Who said 'I have nothing to declare except my genius' and when did he say it?" asked the quizmaster.

Sometimes you may need to use two sets of inverted commas in one sentence. This happens when you write a title or quote someone's words in the middle of a sentence that is already a quotation. The clearest thing to do is to use double inverted commas for the outer marks and single inverted commas for the inner marks.

Titles

> Use capital letters for the first word and any other important words.

> In printed material titles are often put in italics.

> Have you read "The Life and Adventures of Freddy the Frog"?

> Do not use capital letters for words like "a", "the", "and", "of", "at", "to", "in", "from", "on", "for".

You also need to use inverted commas when you write the titles of books, plays, films, newspapers, magazines, poems, songs, paintings and T.V. programmes.

Unusual words

Unusual words such as specialist terms, foreign words, slang and words used only in certain areas are often put in inverted commas. This helps to show the reader that they are unusual (and that the reader is not necessarily expected to know it already).

> He "flipped his lid".

> We stayed in a small "pension".

> The wind is "veering" when it changes in a clockwise direction.

Being funny

> Our "luxury" hotel turned out to be a concrete shed surrounded by a field of mud.

Inverted commas can help you to add an ironical, sarcastic or funny twist to something you write. You can put them round some words to give the word emphasis and show that you do not take it seriously.

Words quoted for discussion

> I have looked up "amnesia" in the dictionary hundreds of times, but I always forget what it means.

When you write a word, not simply for its meaning within a sentence, but in order to say something particular about it, you should put it in inverted commas.

Spot the title

Where should the inverted commas go?

1. He went to see Superman and E.T. last week.
2. They had good reviews in The Times.
3. I wanted to watch Coronation Street and Dallas so I didn't go with him.

15

*For apostrophes, see page 23.

Colons and semi-colons

Colons and semi-colons, like commas and full stops, mark the places where you would break or pause when speaking. You can get away without using them, but they can come in useful and it is worth knowing where you can use them.

Imagine that each punctuation mark has a certain strength according to how long a pause it represents. The comma is the weakest mark; then comes the semi-colon. The colon is stronger than the semi-colon, but weaker than the full stop.

Old-fashioned teachers used to tell their pupils to pause and count one at a comma, two at a semi-colon, three at a colon and four at a full stop. It might sound rather odd if you tried doing this, but it may help you to understand how to use colons and semi-colons.

How colons are used

1 A colon nearly always "introduces" or leads into something that is to follow. You may see it used before someone speaks or before a quotation.

> Don't forget that you have to use inverted commas* as well as colons here.

> **He said: "I'll eat my hat."**

> **Remember the saying: "A stitch in time saves nine."**

2 A colon is used to break a sentence when the second half of the sentence explains, expands or summarizes what comes in the first half.

> **Eventually he told us his secret: the old beggar was, in fact, a very rich man.**

> A colon used like this often means the same as "that is to say".

3 Colons are also used to introduce lists. Some people use a dash after the colon at the beginning of a list, but it is better to leave the dash out.

> **To make this pudding you will need the following ingredients: three ripe bananas, a pint of fresh cream, a small glass of brandy and some cherries and almonds for decoration.**

> Watch out for these phrases. All of them are quite often followed by a colon.

> **for example**
> **in other words**
> **to sum up**
> **the following**
> **as follows**

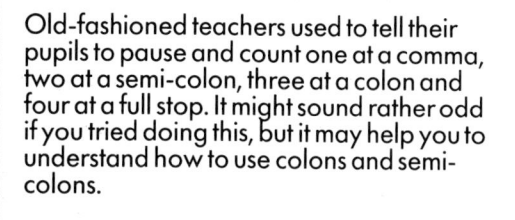

16

*For inverted commas see pages 12-13.

How semi-colons are used

1 A semi-colon can sometimes be used to replace a full stop. It links two complete sentences and turns them into one sentence. The two sentences should be closely linked in meaning and of equal importance.

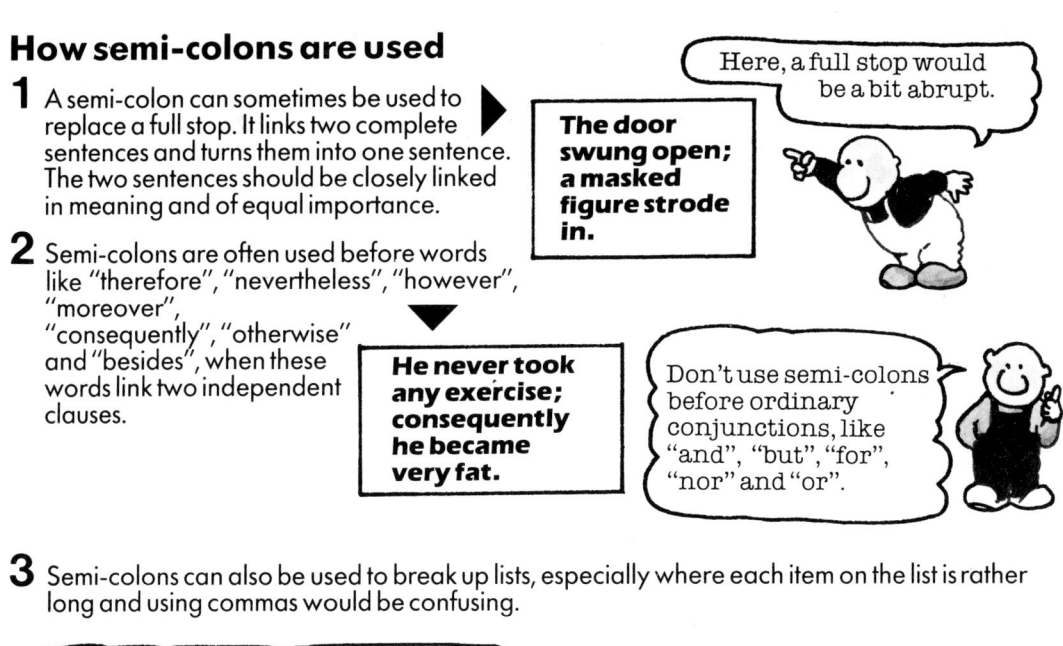

> **The door swung open; a masked figure strode in.**

> Here, a full stop would be a bit abrupt.

2 Semi-colons are often used before words like "therefore", "nevertheless", "however", "moreover", "consequently", "otherwise" and "besides", when these words link two independent clauses.

> **He never took any exercise; consequently he became very fat.**

> Don't use semi-colons before ordinary conjunctions, like "and", "but", "for", "nor" and "or".

3 Semi-colons can also be used to break up lists, especially where each item on the list is rather long and using commas would be confusing.

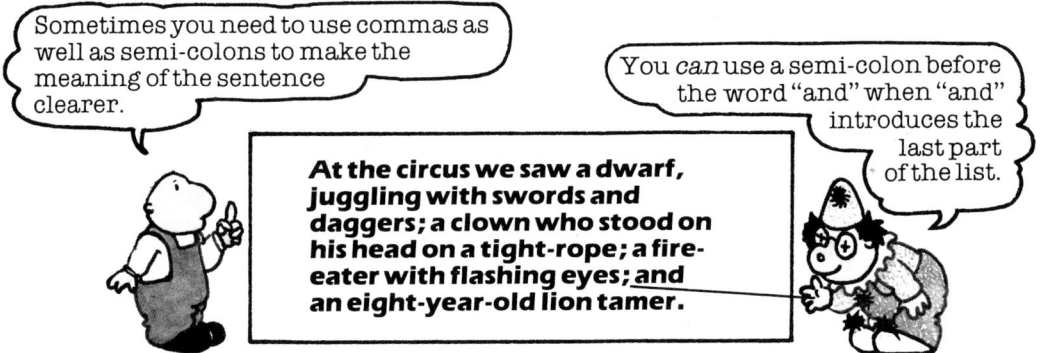

> Sometimes you need to use commas as well as semi-colons to make the meaning of the sentence clearer.

> **At the circus we saw a dwarf, juggling with swords and daggers; a clown who stood on his head on a tight-rope; a fire-eater with flashing eyes; and an eight-year-old lion tamer.**

> You *can* use a semi-colon before the word "and" when "and" introduces the last part of the list.

Deciding which one to use

If the first part of the sentence leads you forward to the information in the second part of the sentence, use a colon.

If the two parts of the sentence seem to be equally balanced, use a semi-colon.

There are times when it is difficult to decide whether to use a colon or a semi-colon.

> **The boy was like his father: short, fat and with a large nose.**

> **Florence was very keen on swimming; her sister preferred cycling.**

Do	Use a colon: 1. Before a list. 2. To introduce an explanation, expansion or summary of the first part of the sentence.	Use a semi-colon: 1. To join two closely linked sentences. 2. To break up lists.

Don't	Use a capital letter after either a colon or a semi-colon.

17

Brackets and dashes

Brackets are used in pairs around a group of words to keep them separate from the rest of the sentence. The words inside the brackets can also be referred to as "in parenthesis".

Brackets always appear in pairs.

I spoke to Eliza (her sister is a doctor) about your strange symptoms.

The streets were deserted (it was Easter Sunday) and not a single shop was open.

I gave the bear a banana (all I had left).

Interruption.

Explanation.

Afterthought.

If you take away the words between the brackets, the rest of the sentence should still make complete sense.

The words marked off by brackets introduce an extra idea into the sentence. This extra idea could be an explanation of something else in the sentence, an afterthought, or an interruption of the main idea in the sentence.

Full stops and commas with brackets

When you use brackets it is sometimes difficult to decide exactly where to put commas, full stops and other punctuation marks. First work out how you would punctuate the sentence if the words in brackets were not there.

(you all know what we have to do)

The rescue is tomorrow, but the plans may be changed any time.

A comma would normally come after the second bracket not before the first one.

We will need to take plenty of provisions (blankets, clothes, food and weapons).

If the words in brackets come at the end of a sentence, a full stop comes after the second bracket.

Wake me early. (Set your alarms for five o'clock.) We must leave before it gets light.

If the words in the brackets make a complete sentence and come between complete sentences, put a full stop inside the second bracket.

Double dashes

Dashes can be used in pairs, like brackets, to separate a group of words from the rest of a sentence. They are only used if the words they separate come in the middle of a sentence.

You could use brackets here.

Hannah invited her friends – there were ten boys and ten girls – to a fancy dress party.

Test yourself on brackets

These sentences need brackets to make sense. Can you think where they should go?

1. She got up early to go shopping the sales were on.
2. She went with Anne her best friend and the lady next door.
3. It took ages to travel home there was a bus strike and they returned exhausted.

Single dashes

Dashes, unlike brackets, do not always have to be used in pairs. For certain purposes they can be used singly. In some situations they are an alternative to brackets but they can also be used to mark an expectant pause.

1
> **They tell me he is very kind – I don't know him.**

You could use brackets here.

A dash is often used to mark a pause or break before a sudden change of direction in a sentence. It may come before an afterthought added on to the end of a sentence.

2
List.

> **Apples, pears, plums – all these grow in our orchard.**

You could use brackets here.

Summary.   Summary.

> **My favourite kind of fruit is citrus fruit – oranges, grapefruits, lemons, limes.**

List.

Sometimes a dash is used to separate a list from its summary. The summary may come before or after the list.

3
Pause for dramatic effect.

> **I opened the lid eagerly and there inside the box was – a dead mouse.**

The part of the sentence after the dash is often surprising or unexpected. The dash gives you a moment of suspense before the surprise.

4
You could use brackets here.

> **The jumper she made was full of mistakes – mistakes which you could see at a glance.**

Sometimes you may want to emphasize a particular word in a sentence by repeating it. If you do this, use a dash to separate the two identical words.

*For commas see pages 8-9.

Choosing between brackets and dashes

When you want to put words in parenthesis you have to choose whether to use brackets or dashes. This often depends on which you happen to prefer. If you can't decide, think about how strong a division you want to make between the words in parenthesis and the rest of the sentence.

Brackets mark the strongest division.

Dashes mark a less strong division.

If the words you want to separate are fairly close to the main meaning of the sentence, a pair of commas* may do the job quite well.

If you are still in doubt, it is probably safest to use brackets.

Practise your dashes

Where should the dashes go?

1. She decided to emigrate to Canada I don't know why.
2. She packed everything she could think of clothes, jewellery, books and records.
3. They drove on and on up the hill until at last, there to her delight was a beautiful old house.

Don't

1. Use double dashes if the parenthesis comes at the end of a sentence. Do use brackets or a single dash.
2. Use more than one pair of dashes in the same sentence.
3. Use double dashes and a single dash in the same sentence.
4. Put brackets within brackets.

Do

1. Use brackets or dashes to separate an interruption, explanation or afterthought from the main sentence.

19

Hyphens

The hyphen is half the length of a dash. It is a linking mark which joins two or more words together to make one word or expression.

Compound words

1 When two or more words are joined together they are called compound words. They can be compound nouns or compound adjectives.

water

wheel

This is a compound noun.

water-wheel

He gave her a **five-pound** box of chocolates.

This is a compound adjective.

2 Sometimes the compound word is made up of a noun or an adjective and a participle. A hyphen is used to join these.

This is a participle.

short-sighted
hard-wearing
home-made

The kind-hearted old lady gave five pots of home-made jam to the bazaar.

3 A hyphen is used to join an adjective or noun to a noun ending in d or ed.

blue-eyed

heavy-footed

She had a blue-eyed, big-eared, bird-brained boyfriend.

4 You can use a hyphen to make a group of words into an expression.

do-it-yourself

good-for-nothing

The do-it-yourself man was a bit happy-go-lucky!

5 You also use a hyphen to write numbers and fractions that are more than one word.

three-quarters
sixty-six

When she reached the age of twenty-one Cynthia inherited three-quarters of her father's money.

Nine missing... have a go!

There are nine hyphens missing. Where should they go?

The half witted taxi driver was ninety nine years old and had rather a couldn't care less attitude. This resulted in the hard working woman arriving tear stained and miserable three quarters of an hour late for the dress rehearsal.

Avoiding confusion

6 When the meaning of something is vague you can use a hyphen to avoid confusion.

> Man eating tiger escapes from the zoo.

> This is what is really meant.

> Man-eating tiger escapes from the zoo.

| a walking-stick | not | a walking stick |

7 Two words can be spelt exactly the same way and have different meanings. Sometimes a hyphen is used to make the difference clear.

| recover re-cover | resign re-sign |

She re-covered the sofa when she had recovered from her illness.

8 When two words are joined together and have identical letters they are separated by a hyphen.

re-echo *not* reecho

This looks odd.

Never write this.

grass-seed *not* grassseed

9 A hyphen can be used to attach a prefix to a word. This changes the meaning of the word.

This is a prefix.

**pre-school
ex-army
multi-storey
anti-aircraft**

10

The man fell overboard and the ship sailed on. He sank beneath the gigantic waves and was never seen again.

Sometimes a word must be broken at the end of a line because it is too long to fit in completely. When this happens you can use a hyphen to divide the word.
Try to break the word so that neither too much nor too little is left and it is still easy to read as one word.

If in doubt

Some words that were once hyphenated are now accepted as one word. If you are doubtful about when to use a hyphen always use a dictionary.

**nightdress
inkwell
haystack**

Try again

Can you see where the hyphens should go here?

Her father was an ex army officer who was injured in the war. Although he was a semi invalid he was self reliant and sat all day at his writing desk typing out novels non stop.

Apostrophes

An apostrophe looks like a comma only it is raised off the line of writing. It is used for various reasons.

1 Showing who owns what (possession)

An apostrophe goes after the owner's name to show something belongs to him or her.

This shows the cat belongs to Jane.

If the owner is singular, put the apostrophe at the end of the word and add an "s".

This is Jane's cat.

If the word ends in an "s" already you still need an apostrophe + another "s".

That is James's dog.

When the owner is plural (more than one) and the word ends in "s" already just put the apostrophe after the "s" that is already there.

Just the apostrophe here.

The man stole the ladies' handbags.

If the plural does not end in "s" you still add an apostrophe + "s".

Apostrophe "s".

Take care! There is *no* apostrophe with these possessive pronouns.

He went to get the men's coats.

| its | his | hers | ours | yours |

2 Filling in for missing letters (contractions)

You can also use an apostrophe when you want to leave out one or more letters. The apostrophe goes in where the letters come out. In this way two words are joined together in a shorter form. These are called *contractions*.

she has	she's
you are	you're
I am	I'm	we have	we've

There are some unusual contractions.

| shall not – shan't <br> will not – won't
 I would – I'd | I had – I'd <br> of the clock – o'clock |

Don't confuse *it's* and *its*.
it's — it is
      it has
its —this is the possessive pronoun.

| It's time we all went to bed. (It is) | It's been a long day. (It has) |

The cat wants its supper.

There is nothing missing here.

Watch out for *who's* and *whose*. These sound the same but they are different.

| Who's coming with us? (Who is) | Whose book is that? (To whom does that book belong?) |

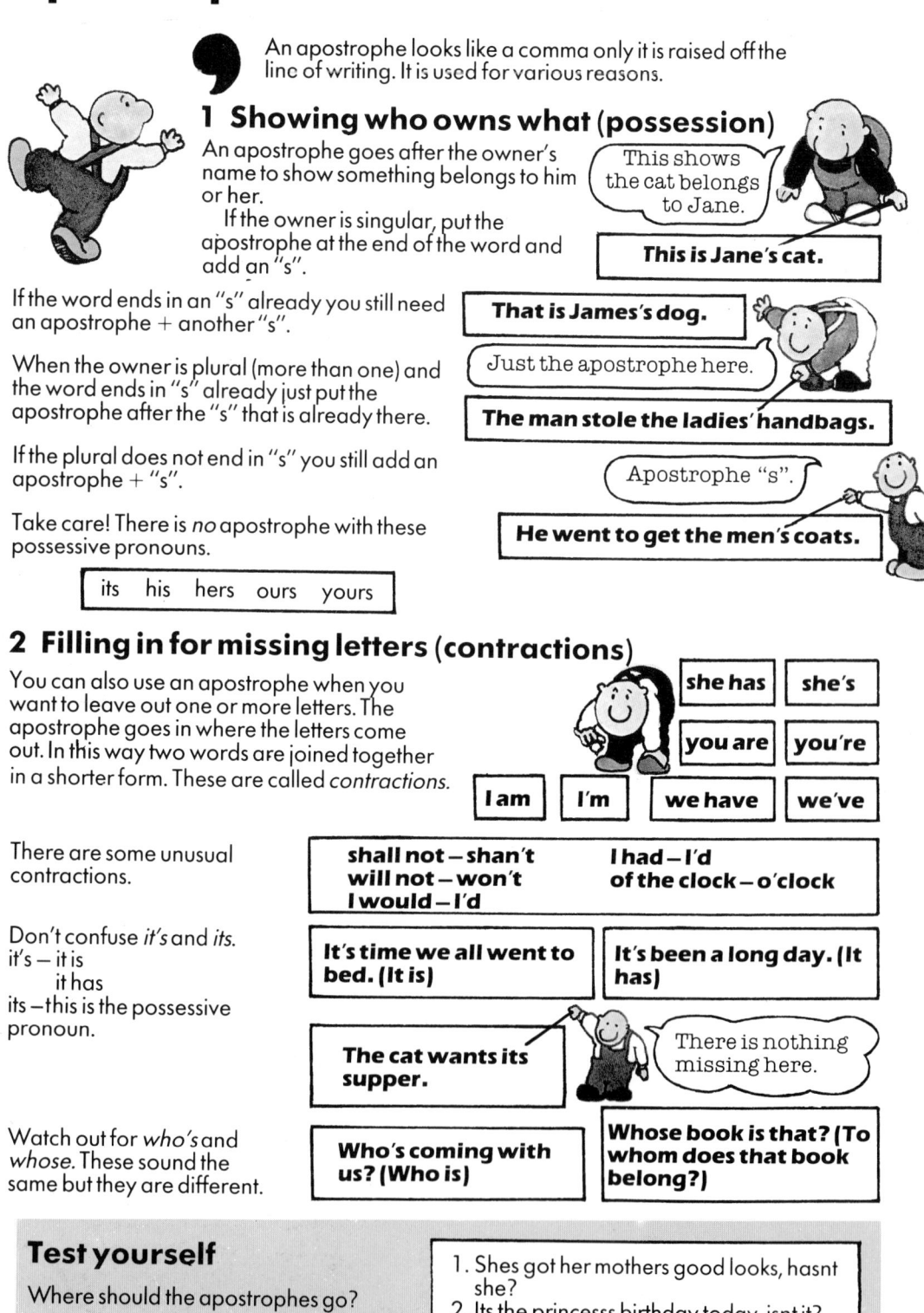

Capital letters

A capital letter should always be used for:

1 The beginning of a sentence.

> **The old lady took her dog for a walk.**

2 People's names.

> **Henrietta** **Bert** **Doris Smith**
>
> Surnames and Christian names.

3 Names of places.

> **New York** **Mount Everest** **River Thames**
>
> These can be towns, cities, countries, rivers or lakes.

But don't use capitals for the points of the compass —

> **north** **south** **east** **west**

unless it is part of the name.

> **North Pole** **South Africa**

4 Names of streets, roads and buildings.

> **Church Road** **Main Street**
>
> **Empire State Building**

5 Titles of books, plays, songs, newspapers, films and poems.

> **The Spy Who Loved Me** **The Mousetrap**

6 Days of the week, months of the year and for special days.

> **Monday** **December** **Christmas**

But capitals are not used for the seasons of the year.

> **spring** **winter** **summer** **autumn**
>
> No capitals here.

7 A capital letter is used for titles.

> **Prime Minister** **Admiral-of-the-Fleet**

8 Also for titles before names.

> **Lord Longford** **Prince Charles**

But these titles do not have capitals when they do not accompany a name.

> No capital here.
>
> **The Duke of York made a speech. Afterwards the duke walked out.**

9 The name of God, Jesus Christ and words relating to them have capitals.

> **The Messiah** **Our Father** **Allah**

10 The word I is always a capital. It must never be a small letter.

> **I think I am going to be sick.**

11 Capitals are always used to begin paragraphs and to start each new line of an address.

> Capitals here.
>
> Dr A. Giles,
> The Farthings,
> Cheam.
> Surrey.

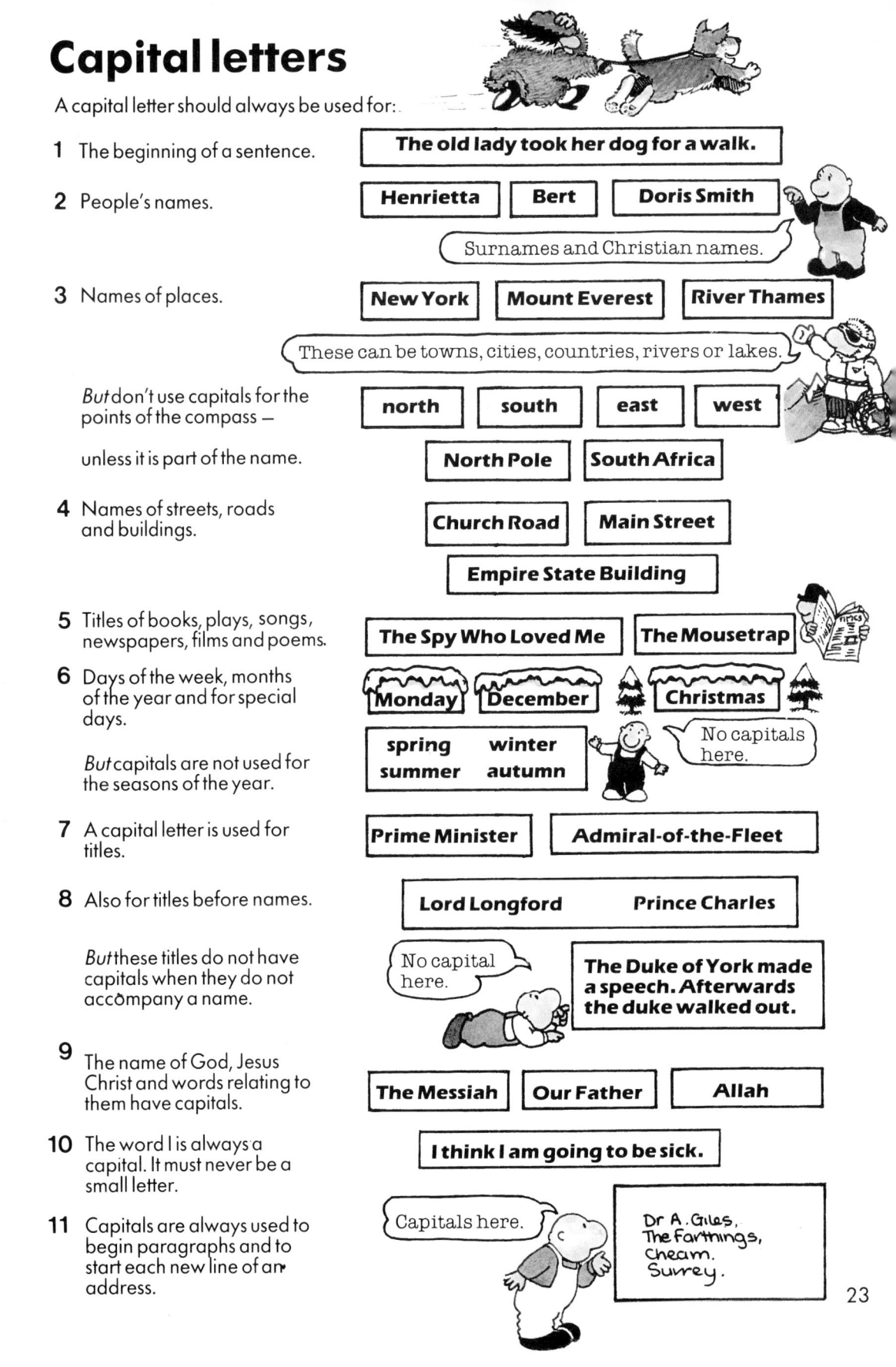

23

Layout

Just as punctuation helps a reader to understand what you have written, the way you arrange words on a page and the amount of space you leave around them, also helps your reader to understand and take in the exact meaning of your words.

Paragraphs

Long chunks of writing unbroken by paragraphs are very offputting to most readers. A paragraph is a set of sentences. There are no hard and fast rules about how many sentences there should be in a paragraph. Use as many as makes an easily digestible piece of reading, but try to end one paragraph and begin another at a point where it is logical to have a slight break.

The first line of a paragraph is set inwards from the margin (indented) to make it easier to see where each paragraph begins.

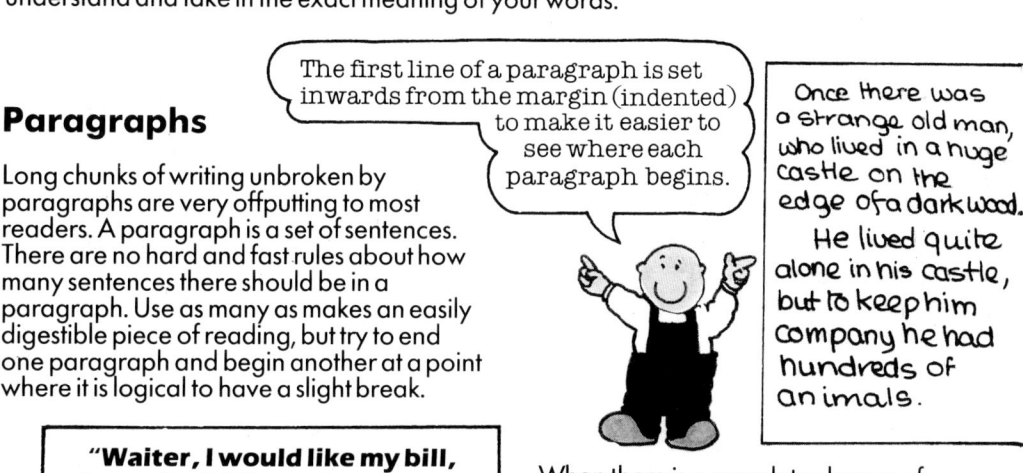

Once there was a strange old man, who lived in a huge castle on the edge of a dark wood.

He lived quite alone in his castle, but to keep him company he had hundreds of animals.

> "Waiter, I would like my bill, please," said the customer.
> "How did you find your steak, sir?" asked the waiter.
> "Ah, I just moved the potato and there it was."

When you write down conversations you start a new paragraph every time one person stops speaking and another person starts. This makes it much easier for the reader to tell who is speaking which words.

When there is a complete change of subject it is usually quite easy to tell that a new paragraph is needed. If you are telling a story, the following occasions might be the right moment for a new paragraph:
1. When a person is introduced into the story.
2. When a new place is introduced into the story.
3. When there is a change of time.

Letters

There is a special pattern to follow when you write letters, which helps to make them much clearer to the reader. Below you can see one way of setting out your letters to friends or relatives.

Remember to put a comma here.

Your own address. You can indent each line, as shown here, or start each line straight below the one above.

Put commas at the end of each line and a full stop at the end of the last line.

Here are some other endings you can use in personal letters:
Love from,
With love,
Yours ever,
Best wishes,

The date goes below the address.

Remember to put a comma after your ending.

Leave a margin on both sides of the writing and a space at the top and bottom of the page.

Write your ending and signature in the middle or slightly to the right.

33, New Rd,
Clinton,
Beds,
U2 R1
23rd June 1993.

Dear Rob,
Just a short note to let you know that I'll be able to arrange the reunion for the 14th September. I will keep you informed.

Yours sincerely,

Sonia Head.

Test yourself

Put in the capitals

Can you see where they should go?

There should be 19 capital letters below.

Try not to write in the book. Use paper instead.

at christmastime harriet and tom brown went to london to stay with their uncle william. their uncle was admiral-of-the-fleet in the royal navy and he had some very grand friends. while the children were staying he had a party, to which he invited the prime minister, the duke of monmouth and a famous author from america.

Apostrophes

Where should the missing apostrophes go?

1. Its the first time this week that the dog has eaten its food.
2. Toms wife is Jamess sister.
3. The ladies cloakroom is next to the mens.
4. Shes a lot older than she looks.
5. Weve not forgotten that youre an excellent cook.
6. Whose turn is it to see whos coming?

Can you shorten this conversation using apostrophes?

"I am tired," said Fred. "I have had an awful day." "Where have you been?" asked his mother. "It is late, and we have been looking everywhere for you. You are lucky we did not call the police. I will not give you any supper until I know what is going on."

Spot the missing hyphens

There are 16 hyphens missing below. Can you see where they should go?

1. The girl with reddish brown hair kept teasing Ben, but as he was rather thick skinned and happy go lucky it didn't bother him.
2. The half witted man drove three quarters of the way in the wrong direction. He went south east instead of north west.
3. The hard working old lady had a well earned rest when she retired at the age of sixty five.
4. As her six foot tall fiancé was rather a ne'er do well, the twenty one year old girl broke off their nine month long engagement.

Colon or semi-colon?

Can you decide where to put a colon or semi-colon?

1. Many people wear uniforms to work policemen, nurses, traffic wardens, bus drivers and schoolchildren.
2. Alice never had enough to eat therefore she became thin and ill.
3. Tom worked long hours every day nevertheless he remained healthy.
4. The actor read aloud "To be, or not to be that is the question."
5. There was a knock at the door in came a tall, hooded figure.
6. At last he told us everything he had been involved in the most horrific murder.

Brackets, dashes or commas?

Can you think where to put brackets, dashes or commas to make these sentences clearer?

1. Maud took all her family three boys and three girls to the cinema.
2. They all have names beginning with the letter J Joshua, Jeremy, John, Joanne, Jessica and Jane.
3. Joanne the youngest ate three boxes of popcorn.
4. Joshua unlike the others ate nothing the whole time.
5. Poor Maud had no money left it cost £1.50 each to get in.

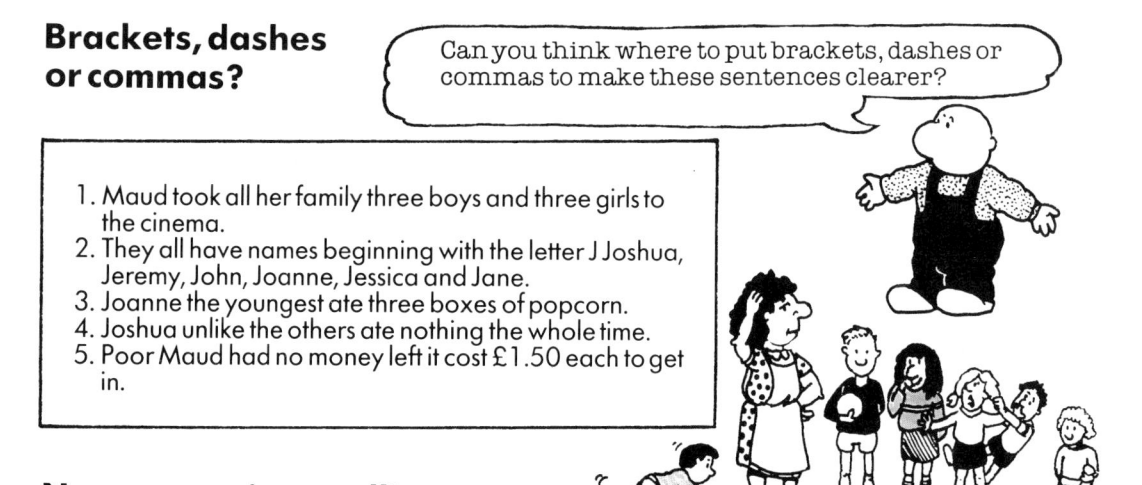

No punctuation at all!

Can you rewrite this conversation putting in the capital letters, full stops, commas, inverted commas, question marks, exclamation marks and anything else you think necessary?

theres a letter for you called her mother ive put it on the table
amanda rushed down the stairs tore open the envelope and
found to her delight it was an invitation
hooray ive been invited to jamess twenty first birthday party she
cried there was a pause what am i going to wear
youve got plenty of clothes dear replied her mother calmly sipping
her tea theres absolutely nothing suitable for jamess party
amanda replied it will be very smart
whats james like asked her mother suspiciously
hes six foot tall with brownish blond hair huge brown eyes and a
wonderful smile replied amanda
her mother sighed i meant what is his personality like is he hard
working trustworthy kind and clever or is he selfish and mean

27

Now turn over and see if you were right.

Answers

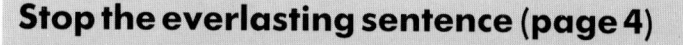

Stop the everlasting sentence (page 4)

He trudged wearily along the dusty road. His feet hurt and his head throbbed. There was not a soul in sight for miles and he wondered what to do next. Then he saw someone waving at him at the top of the hill. It was a tall man with a large hat.

Short or long? (page 5)

V.C.	Automobile Association
etc.	or Alcoholics Anynomous
Rev. J. Williams	Royal Automobile Club
Prof. A. Johnson	or Royal Armoured Corps
St. Augustine	Young Women's Christian Association
cm	Royal Society for the Prevention of
	Cruelty to Animals
	Women's Royal Voluntary Service
	Saint John, Chapter 4, verse 3
	Bachelor of Science

Question quiz (page 6)

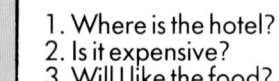

1. Where is the hotel?
2. Is it expensive?
3. Will I like the food?
4. It's a large room, isn't it?
5. How long shall I stay?

Try these (page 8)

1. The monster was huge, fat and spiky.
2. Everyone threw spears, stones, swords and boiling oil at the creature.
3. It roared, growled, spat and groaned, but still it did not die.
4. A knight appeared wearing bright, shining armour and pierced the beast with his special, magic sword.
5. The huge beast screamed, fell to the ground, rolled over and died.
6. The king rewarded the knight with gold, silver, diamonds, rubies and other precious things.

Test yourself (page 9)

1. The robber climbed through the window, crept up the stairs and peered into the bedroom.
2. She called as loudly as she could, but no-one could hear her.
3. The telephone was not far away, yet there was little she could do to reach it.
4. She quickly switched on all the lights, so the man ran away in a panic.
5. The policeman, who arrived later, told her to put a lock on her window.

Puzzle it out (page 10)

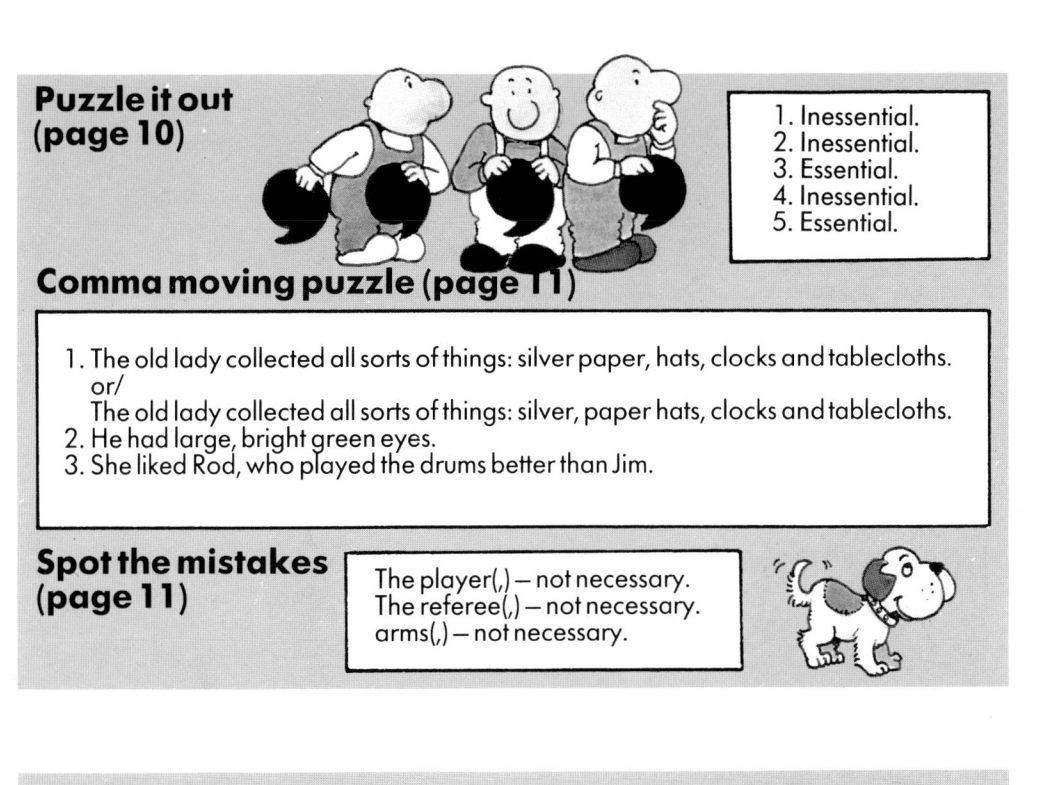

1. Inessential.
2. Inessential.
3. Essential.
4. Inessential.
5. Essential.

Comma moving puzzle (page 11)

1. The old lady collected all sorts of things: silver paper, hats, clocks and tablecloths.
   or/
   The old lady collected all sorts of things: silver, paper hats, clocks and tablecloths.
2. He had large, bright green eyes.
3. She liked Rod, who played the drums better than Jim.

Spot the mistakes (page 11)

The player(,) — not necessary.
The referee(,) — not necessary.
arms(,) — not necessary.

Turn nonsense into a conversation (page 14)

"Good morning, how are you today?" the doctor asked.

"I feel dreadful," he replied gruffly.

"You should try to get up and walk about," she suggested. "Then you might feel better."

"You must be joking!" he exclaimed. "Do you want a patient or a corpse?"

Spot the title (page 15)

1. He went to see "Superman" and "E.T." last week.
2. They had good reviews in "The Times".
3. I wanted to watch "Coronation Street" and "Dallas" so I didn't go with him.

Test yourself on brackets (page 18)

1. She got up early to go shopping (the sales were on).
2. She went with Anne (her best friend) and the lady next door.
3. It took ages to get home (there was a bus strike), and they returned exhausted.

Practise your dashes (page 19)

1. She decided to emigrate to Canada — I don't know why.
2. She packed everything she could think of — clothes, jewellery, books and records.
3. They drove on and on up the hill until at last, there to her delight was — a beautiful old house.

How well have you done?

Nine missing . . . have a go! (page 20)

The half-witted taxi-driver was ninety-nine years old and had rather a couldn't-care-less attitude. This resulted in the hard-working woman arriving tear-stained and miserable three-quarters of an hour late for the dress-rehearsal.

Try again (page 21)

Her father was an ex-army officer who was injured in the war. Although he was a semi-invalid he was self-reliant and sat all day at his writing-desk typing out novels non-stop.

Test yourself (page 22)

1. She's got her mother's good looks, hasn't she?
2. It's the princess's birthday today, isn't it?
3. The women's Keep Fit Class opens today.

Put in the capitals (page 26)

At Christmastime Harriet and Tom Brown went to London to stay with their Uncle William. Their uncle was Admiral-of-the-Fleet in the Royal Navy and he had some very grand friends. While the children were staying he had a party, to which he invited the Prime Minister, the Duke of Monmouth and a famous author from America. (19 capitals)

Apostrophes (page 26)

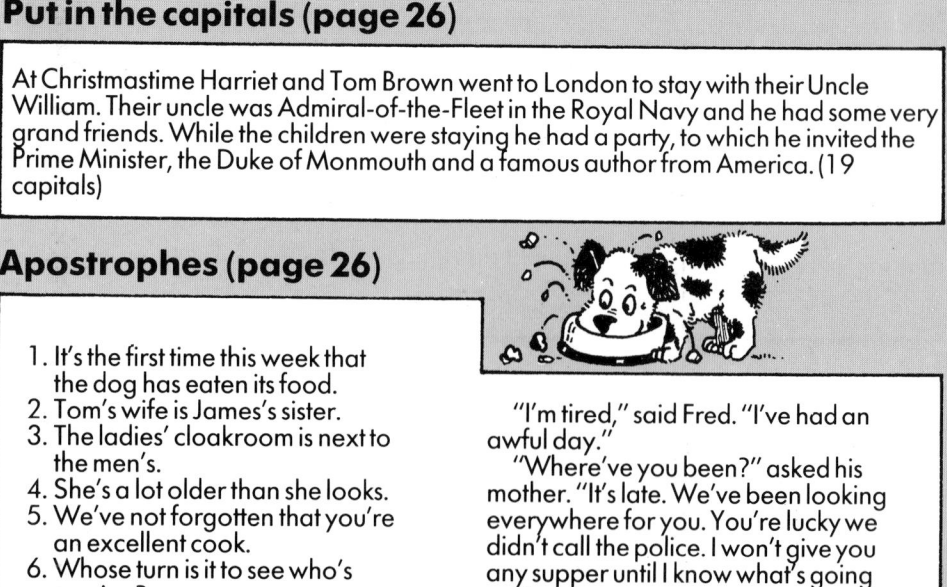

1. It's the first time this week that the dog has eaten its food.
2. Tom's wife is James's sister.
3. The ladies' cloakroom is next to the men's.
4. She's a lot older than she looks.
5. We've not forgotten that you're an excellent cook.
6. Whose turn is it to see who's coming?

"I'm tired," said Fred. "I've had an awful day."

"Where've you been?" asked his mother. "It's late. We've been looking everywhere for you. You're lucky we didn't call the police. I won't give you any supper until I know what's going on."

Spot the missing hyphens

1. The girl with reddish-brown hair kept teasing Ben, but as he was rather thick-skinned and happy-go-lucky it didn't bother him.
2. The half-witted man drove three-quarters of the way in the wrong direction. He went south-east instead of north-west.
3. The hard-working old lady had a well-earned rest when she retired at the age of sixty-five.
4. As her six-foot tall fiancé was rather a n'er-do-well, the twenty-one year old girl broke off their nine-month long engagement. (16 hyphens)

(page 27)

Colon or semi-colon?

1. Many people wear uniforms to work: policemen, nurses, traffic wardens, bus drivers and schoolchildren.
2. Alice never had enough to eat; therefore she became thin and ill.
3. Tom worked long hours every day; nevertheless he remained healthy.
4. The actor read aloud: "To be, or not to be: that is the question."
5. There was a knock at the door: in came a tall, hooded figure.
6. At last he told us everything: he had been involved in the most horrific murder.

Brackets, dashes or commas?

1. Maud took all her family — three boys and three girls — to the cinema.
2. They all have names beginning with the letter J — Joshua, Jeremy, John, Joanne, Jessica and Jane.
3. Joanne (the youngest) ate three boxes of popcorn.
4. Joshua, unlike the others, ate nothing the whole time.
5. Poor Maud had no money left (it cost £1.50 each to get in).

No punctuation at all! (page 27)

"There's a letter for you," called her mother. "I've put it on the table."

Amanda rushed down the stairs, tore open the envelope and found to her delight — it was an invitation.

"Hooray! I've been invited to James's twenty-first birthday party," she cried. There was a pause. "What am I going to wear?"

"You've got plenty of clothes, dear," replied her mother, calmly sipping her tea.

"There's absolutely nothing suitable for James's party," Amanda replied. "It will be very smart."

"What's James like?" asked her mother suspiciously.

"He's six-foot tall with brownish-blond hair, huge brown eyes and a wonderful smile," replied Amanda.

Her mother sighed. "I meant what is his personality like? Is he hard-working, trustworthy, kind and clever; or is he selfish, and mean?"

Index/glossary

adjective, 9, 20 Describing word which gives a fuller meaning to a noun: e.g. *pretty* girl, *vicious* dog.

apostrophe, 15, 22 Punctuation mark which shows: (1) that one or more letters have been missed out; e.g. didn't; (2) possession.

brackets, 18 Two punctuation marks used to enclose words or figures to separate them from the main part of the text.

capital letters, 4, 12, 23 Upper case letters used: (1) to start a sentence; (2) for proper nouns e.g. people's names.

clause, 9 Subdivision of a sentence which includes a verb. There are two kinds: (1) main clause; (2) subordinate clause. The main clause makes complete sense on its own, but a subordinate clause is dependent on the main clause for its sense: e.g. He ate a loaf of bread, (main clause) because he was hungry. (subordinate clause).

colon, 17 Mark of punctuation usually used before a quotation or contrast of ideas.

comma, 8, 9, 10, 11, 13, 16, 18 Punctuation mark representing shortest pause in a sentence.

compound word, 20 Word made up from two or more other words.

conjunction, 9, 17 Word which connects words, clauses or sentences.

contraction, 22 Shortened form of two words, using an apostrophe.

dash, 19 Punctuation mark which marks a pause or break in the sense of the text.

direct question, 6 The kind of question which expects an answer in return.

direct speech, 12 The exact words that someone speaks.

exclamation mark, 4, 7 Punctuation mark used at the end of a sentence or phrase, when the content conveys a strong feeling or emotion.

full stop, 4, 5, 16, 18 Strongest punctuation mark making the most definite pause. Used at the end of all sentences which are not questions or exclamations.

hyphen, 20, 21 Punctuation mark used to link two or more words together to make one word or expression.

indirect question, 6 This kind of sentence does not ask a question but tells you what question was asked.

inverted commas, 12, 13, 14, 15 Punctuation marks used to show the exact words that someone has spoken.

noun, 4, 20 Word used as the name of a person, thing or place: e.g. dog, man.

paragraph, 23, 24 Passage or section of writing marked off by indenting the first line.

parenthesis, 18 Another word for brackets. Words inside brackets are also called parenthesis.

participle, 20 Part of verb. Can be past or present. (1) Present participle is part of verb that usually ends in *ing*: e.g. making, laughing, working; (2) past participle is the part of the verb which follows "have" or "has" in the past tense: e.g. They have *eaten*. He has *made* it.

phrase, 10 Small group of words without a verb, which is not a complete sentence.

prefix, 21 Small addition to a word made by joining on one or more letters at the beginning. e.g. ex, pre, anti.

pronoun, 22 Word which stands instead of a noun. There are many kinds of pronoun including *possessive* pronouns (mine, yours, hers).

question marks, 4, 6 Punctuation mark used at the end of a sentence which asks a question.

quotation, 4, 14, 16 One or more words or sentences borrowed from another piece of text.

reported speech, 12 Repeating or "reporting" in your own words what someone has said.

semi-colon, 16 Punctuation mark indicating a longer pause than a comma, but less than a colon or full stop.

sentences, 4, 9 A word or group of words which make complete sense on their own.

subordinate, 9 (see clause).

verb, 4 Word which shows some kind of action or being: e.g. run, jump, think, is, was, were.

verb of saying, 13 Verb which is another way of expressing "says" or "said" depending on the context: e.g. whisper, mutter, etc. Usually comes before or after speech in inverted commas: e.g. "Who are you?" she *asked*.

First published in 1983 by Usborne Publishing Ltd, Usborne House, 83-85 Saffron Hill, London EC1N 8RT, England.

© 1990, 1983 Usborne Publishing

 Printed in China